Corn Snake Care

The Complete Guide to Caring for and Keeping Corn Snakes as Pets

Tabitha Jones

ISBN: 9781799032854

CONTENTS

INTRODUCTION

Before purchasing any pet it is important to understand that as a pet owner you are responsible for the care and wellbeing of your pet. It is important to try and learn as much as you can about the animal you are considering to keep as a pet to make sure that your lifestyle, household and financial status are suited to provide your pet with the best possible care. This guide has been designed to provide you with both precise and concise information about a corn snake's basic needs to help you provide your pet with the best quality care practices.

DESCRIPTION

The corn snake (scientifically known as *Pantherophis guttatus*) is a species of nonvenomous rat snake that subdues its prey through constriction. The species gained the name 'corn snake' due to the fact that they regularly hunt around grain stores to catch mice and rats who are attracted by the harvest. However some people argue that the species is named after 'corn' due to the fact that the patterning on the snakes body somewhat resembles the kernels of variegated corn. This resemblance is furthered due to the fact that the species most common colour morph is a mixture of oranges and yellows. Unfortunately the corn snake resembles the venomous copperhead and is therefore often killed as a result of this. The corn snake is a North American species but can also be commonly found throughout the southeastern and more central states of the United States.

Size

Males normally range between 3 and 6ft. Females tend to be larger than males. Females normally range between 4 and 6ft. However adult Corn Snakes have been known to grow over 6ft in length!.

Lifespan

The life span of a captive corn snake is between 10 to 15 years – although they have been known to live for as long as 20 years! It is important to consider the life span of the snake before purchase to make sure that you are financially stable enough and committed enough to provide the snake with care for the entirety of its life.

Natural Habitat

In the wild corn snakes prefer habitats such as forest floors, trees, abandoned buildings or farmhouses and over grown fields. Juvenile corn snakes tend to spend their first four months living at ground level and after this age it is not uncommon to find them in the branches of trees. As previously mentioned corn snakes are native to the United States and can be found mainly in the south eastern states such as New Jersey to the Florida Keys. They are also not uncommon in more southern states such as Texas.

Diet

Like all snakes, the corn snake is a carnivorous species and will need to hunt for food every few days. In the wild, their diet mainly consists of small mammals – mainly rodents such as rats, mice and shrews. However they are also known to consume birds or bird eggs if they are able to get them. It is not uncommon for corn snakes to also eat amphibians, reptiles or smaller snakes – including smaller corn snakes!

Differences between the Sexes

It is possible to assume the sex of your corn snake based upon the thickness of its tail after the cloacal opening. A female's tail will taper into a point after the cloacal opening whereas a male with have a large section which is of equal width to the cloacal opening before tapering to a point. The reason males have this large thick section is because it is housing their hemipenis. There is only one way to 100% find out your snakes sex and that is through the process of probing. However probing is a controversial topic within the world of herpetology and will therefore be discussed at length in the section below.

Probing

Probing should NEVER be performed by anyone other than a trained vet who has a long history in the MEDICAL care of snakes and lizards. Probing is the process of forcing open the snake's cloacal opening and pulling the lizard's sex organs out and then replacing them inside of the cloacal opening. It is a very risky process that can lead to multiple health problems such as: internal bleeding, bruising of the sex organs, prolapsing of the cloacal opening, damaging of the cloacal opening or intestines and an increased chance of infection. Due to the dangerous nature of probing we feel it is necessary to reiterate the fact that this process should NOT be performed by anyone other than a trained PROFESSIONAL – learning the sex of your corn snake is not worth risking the plethora of health complications probing raises.

CORN SNAKES AS PETS

Corn snakes are commonly bred in captivity and are popular household pets due to their relatively large size in comparison to other snakes, their interesting patterned appearance and their docile temperament. They are highly unlikely to bite and will only do so if severely threatened. They are easy and safe pets to handle, despite their size, and make good pets for both experienced and beginner snake keepers.

Choosing your Corn Snake

I highly recommend always asking to handle the snake before you purchase it. This will allow you to examine the snake for any health or temperament issues before actually parting with money or taking the snake home. A healthy corn snake will look alert, bright eyed and have a flickering tongue during a handling session. The scales of a healthy corn snake should feel smooth and there should be no traces of half shed skin along the snakes body. If you encounter any problems, or have any doubt about the snakes temperament, do not purchase it.

Transporting your Corn Snake

It is important to know how to correctly transport

your snake as you will need to transport it after purchase and for any visits to the vet. Corn snakes can be easily transported over short distances. Common ways to transport them include plastic tubs with lids or cotton bags which can be tied at the top. Most professional reptile stockiest will provide you with a container to transport the snake but it is worth checking beforehand with both commercial and private sellers. For added comfort, and to further avoid injury, you can line the container with absorbent and soft paper. It is important to keep the transportation container warm. A good way to keep the temperature of the container warm is to use a heat pack during the transportation process. It is best practice to keep transit time to a minimum to reduce the chance of your snake becoming stressed.

Handling

As corn snakes are a somewhat timid species it is common for them to not appreciate being handled for long periods of time. It is recommended to not handle your snake for longer than 15 minutes per handling session. Regular handling is an enjoyable activity for both the snake and owner and also helps to minimize stress during enclosure cleaning and trips to the vet. Another benefit of regular handling is the fact that it allows your corn snake time to exercise outside of its vivarium. Despite being large in size they are easy to handle due to their tendency to move slowly. Corn snakes are known to be clumsy snakes which means that you should take care during all handling sessions. A fall from a small height, depending how the snake lands, could critically injure your snake. To avoid dropping your snake it is also advisable to place your free hand below your corn snake to be ready to catch it in case it falls.

Recording

It is highly advisable to keep a record throughout your corn snake's life. By regularly noting down weight, length and feeding patterns you will have a useful resource to help notice any potential problems with your corn snake and to likewise make sure it is in good health.

CAN MULTIPLE CORN SNAKES BE HOUSED TOGETHER?

It is not considered best practice to house multiple corn snakes in the same vivarium as there is the potential for multiple problems. However some owners have housed multiple corn snakes together without any issues. This section will outline the best practices for housing multiple snakes together to help you make the best choice for your individual case.

Potential Dangers

There are numerous dangers of housing multiple corn snakes together. If the snakes being housed together are not of a similar age or size there is the potential for cannibalism. Larger snakes may also dominate food sources and hide spots which may cause stress in the smaller snakes. There is likewise an increased chance of causing stress in one, or multiple, of the snakes due to the close quarters they are forced to live in. Close quarters also means the spread of disease or illness is far more likely – which would potentially mean that you would have to spend twice as much at the vets! There is also the potential for unexpected breeding to occur so it might be best to house snakes of the same sex to avoid this.

Best Practice when Housing Multiple Corn Snakes

If you decide that you do in fact want to house multiple corn snakes together it is important to have a large vivarium to accommodate multiple snakes and give them space to be apart from each other. Likewise it is important to have multiple sufficient hiding spots for the snakes. If the hiding spots are not of equal quality, a snake that is forced to use an inadequate hiding spot consistently may become stressed. If you are choosing to house multiple corn snakes together it is best practice to monitor them closely to make sure that there are no issues. It is best practice to have a spare vivarium ready in case there are issues and you need to separate your snakes. It is safer to house multiple female corn snakes together as males tend to harass especially during the breeding season.

SHEDDING

Corn snakes, like all snakes, periodically shed their outer layer of skin throughout their lives. As a keeper there is nothing to worry about as the shedding process is both natural, painless and important to keep your snake happy and healthy. Young snakes tend to shed their skin more than adult snakes, due to the fact that they are outgrowing their skin, but generally the shedding process happens several times a year.

Blue Eyes and Dull Skin

If your snake's eyes have suddenly turned a bluish grey colour and it's skin has become dull do not worry. These changes are called Preecdysis – anecdotally known as being in the 'blue'. Preecdysis is the name given to the symptoms which indicate that a corn snake is about to shed its skin. During the shedding process your snake may refuse to eat and may not want to be handle. However your snake may have no noticeable change in temperament – it all depends on how the individual snake deals with the process of Preecdysis. During Preecdysis it is advisable to handle your snake with care as their vision is impaired due to the blue grey membrane covering their eyes. It is common for corn snakes to act more defensive during this process due to their lack of vision.

How can you help?

Some snakes will handle the shedding of their skin easily and not need any assistance but if you want to assist your snake with the shedding process you can raise the humidity in your vivarium: this helps the snake loosen its skin. There are two main ways to increase the humidity in your snakes vivarium. Firstly you can put a bowl of warm water into the vivarium which will allow the corn snake to soak itself if desired. The second method to help loosen the snake's skin is to mist the inside of the vivarium with water to help further raise the humidity. Even if your snake does not need assistance with the shedding process they will still appreciate the process being made easier for them. However as previously mentioned assisting your snake is, in most cases, not essential.

Ecdysis

Ecdysis is the name given to the actual process of shedding. This process is characterised by your snake rubbing its head on rocks, or material within the vivarium, to loosen the skin around its head. Once the skin around its head is loose your corn snake will begin to crawl out of the old skin through a process of rolling the skin inside out as it moves. Once the skin has been fully shed it is best practice to remove it as soon as possible due to the fact that shed skin is normally accompanied by excrement.

Unshed Skin

After removing the shed skin from the vivarium it is best to then check your snake for any unshed skin. Pay particular attention to the snakes eye lids and tail as these areas are most common for skin to not fully shed. If there is any skin that has not been shed use a warm towel or tweezers to remove the unshed skin. Removal of the unshed skin will help to avoid infection and damage to the skin tissue bellow it.

A Moist Shelter

A moist shelter can be provided during the shedding process as it provides a higher level of humidity which assists the corn snake in the shedding process. A good example of a moist shelter is a Tupperware container lined with cypress mulch or peat moss to create the moisture. If you are planning on introducing a moist shelter during the shedding process it is imperative to make sure that the humidity level of your vivarium does not change dramatically.

FEEDING

Corn snakes are relatively easy to provide for in terms of food and water which makes them an excellent pet for beginner snake owners. In the wild a corn snake's diet consists of mainly small mammals such as rats, shrews and mice. Corn snakes are notoriously bad eaters as they will refuse food if they are stressed, about to shed, are not being housed in the correct conditions or do not wish to be handled.

Feeding a Hatchling

It is best practice to feed your hatchling corn snake on small mice. They should be fed once every 5-6 days to encourage their growth. Some owners will feed their snakes twice a week, or feed them two mice instead of one, to encourage weight gain and an increase in length.

Feeding an Adult

Adult corn snakes should be fed an adult mouse every 7-10 days. This is not as strict however as the amount a snake should eat is dependent on its size – for example a larger corn snake may require two adult mice instead of one. Other larger prey can be introduced to create a variation in your snake's diet. The most common variations on larger prey normally include: rats, small rabbits and day old chickens.

Live Prey or Frozen?

DO NOT feed your corn snake live prey. Live prey, even a small mouse, can injury your snake. The prey that corn snakes eat normally have sharp teeth or claws and are therefore undesirable as your snake may not want to eat them straight away leaving the prey an opportunity to defend themselves. Shop bought frozen mice, and other rodents, are available at most reptile shops and even general pet shops. The frozen prey can also be purchased on the internet. Frozen prey should be thawed to room temperature before used to feed the snake. DO NOT feed your snake wild rodents. Wild rodents carry parasites and may contain suburban toxins that could harm your snake.

How to Feed

Your corn snake should be fed outside of the vivarium if possible. This eliminates the risk of your snake ingesting any of the substrate used to line your vivarium. If the snake ingests too much substrate it may become unhealthy and may also regurgitate its food. It is best to avoid handling your corn snake for about 48 hours after feeding as they are likely to regurgitate their meal. To feed your snake you should hold the prey item with tweezers and wiggle it in front of your snake. The wiggling motion simulates life and will therefore attract your snakes attention.

Braining a Mouse

If your corn snake seems reluctant to eat, 'braining' a mouse is a good way to encourage feeding. Snakes are attracted to the scent of brain matter. If you cut, or use a needle to poke a hole, into the skull of a mouse to expose its brain tissue it will increase the chance of the snake feeding.

Bad Eaters

You should not be concerned if your snake misses a meal every now and then. Instead of trying to force your snake to eat you should focus on making the snake more comfortable: handle it less, make sure the hides within the vivarium are sufficient and make sure the temperature is correct. Once the snake is anxiety free it should resume eating again. Corn snakes may also be more reluctant to eat during the shedding process. As previously mentioned it is good to keep a record of your snake's weight, length and feeding habits. By keeping a record you can check if your snake is acting abnormally or in a way that is concerning and take it to a vet.

HOUSING

As corn snakes are not highly active there is no need for a large enclosure. Snakes are prone to escape their vivarium's if they are no sealed properly so you must take care when planning their housing. Make sure your vivarium has a tightly fitting lid as corn snakes are strong enough to move loosely fitted lids. If your lid does not fit tightly and you are worried about your snake escaping it is advisable to place something, light enough to not damage the lid but heavy enough, to stop the snake escaping on each corner – a good example of this would be thin hardback books.

The Perfect Size Vivarium

The way to work out the perfect size vivarium is to take the length of your snake and make it equal to the front and one of the sides of the vivarium.

Examples:

A 5ft corn snake would be perfect for a 3ft by 2ft vivarium.

A 3ft corn snake would be perfect for a 2ft by 1ft vivarium.

The Dangers of an Overly Large Vivarium

If a vivarium is too large, or does not contain enough hiding spots, a corn snake is likely to feel stressed as they will feel unsafe. This stress may lead the corn snake to stop eating and become underweight which in turn will cause health problems.

Hiding Spots

By nature all corn snakes want a place to hide and feel secure and will become stressed if this is not provided for them within their vivarium. Hides can range from cardboard boxes to specially designed hides which can be purchased from a pet shop. It does not matter what the hide looks like as long as it is big enough to allow the corn snake to curl up inside it while also not being too big as this will not make your snake feel secure. It is advisable to have multiple hides in your vivarium and to space them out along the temperature line. This allows for the corn snake to rotate between hides to help control its body temperature.

A Place to Climb

Corn snakes will climb anything you put into their vivarium. Most people provide their snakes with branches and plastic plants. Branches that have come from outside will have to be debugged and soaked in a chlorine/water solution before being introduced to the vivarium to avoided contamination which could lead to illness and disease. If in doubt about a product/branch DO NOT introduced it to your vivarium as it is not worth risking the health of your snake for an aesthetically pleasing piece of furniture.

Mix It Up

Corn snakes are highly intelligent and inquisitive creatures. It is therefore advisable to change the layout of your vivarium every now and then. Upon reintroducing your corn snake to the newly furnished vivarium you will notice the snake exploring its new surroundings.

Water Bowl

Corn snakes need fresh water to drink on a daily basis. Water should be provided in a shallow and heavy bowl – to avoid the snake tipping it over. Water bowls must be changed immediately if you notice that the snake has defecated in it. Water bowls as previously mentioned can also help during the shedding process. The water within the bowl can be either cool or warm in temperature – it is important to note that warm water will increase the humidity inside your vivarium.

Cleaning

It is important to keep your vivarium clean as a poorly maintained enclosure can create health risks for your pet. Snake feces should be cleaned as soon as you spot it as it poses the highest risk of disease or parasites. It is best practice to clean your snake's vivarium at least once a month with a reptile-safe disinfectant and then to rinse the vivarium well. It is also important to clean your hands before and after cleaning the vivarium and handling your snake to minimize the chance of infection between both yourself and your pet.

SUBSTRATES

The term Substrate is defined as being the surface or material on which an organism lives, grows or obtains its nourishment. In terms of corn snake care the substrate is what you choose to line your snake's vivarium. There are multiple different substrates available to use in your vivarium.

Aspen Shavings

Aspen shavings are great for lining the floor of your vivarium. A great bonus is that they collect urine and faeces and can easily be scooped out with a dog or cat litter scoop. However Aspen shavings have two flaws. Firstly they have to be replaced once they become dirty. Secondly your corn snake will need to be removed to be fed as they may ingest the shavings by mistake

Note: DO NOT use Cedar or Redwood shavings as they are toxic to snakes.

Beech Chippings

Beech chippings are cheap and readily available from all reptile stores. They are not as absorbent as Aspen shavings and will like need to be removed once they are dirtied. However they come in three different grades – small, medium and large. This allows you to choose which grade best suits your snake. Despite the choice in size of chipping it is still best practice to feed your snake outside of its vivarium to avoid the chance of it ingesting any chippings.

Oatbran and Wheatbran

Although it sounds like a strange choice to line a vivarium both oatbran and wheatbran are great and inexpensive choices. They a very similar aesthetic as wood chippings but have the benefit of being more easily digestible and dramatically cheaper than their wood chipping counterparts.

Newspaper and Paper Towels

Both newspaper and paper towels are easily obtained and inexpensive. They make for good flooring if your snake has a belly injury as they are smooth and do not have any potentially harmful edges. However there is the potential for harmful inks to be present within the paper which make them not ideal for long term use.

Artificial Grass

There are many grades of artificial grass which allows you to choose which best suits your snakes needs. Artificial grass is widely available in hardware stores and ironically the cheapest is normally the best when it comes to lining a vivarium. The cheapest artificial grass tends to be the most flexible which makes it easier to clean and also less likely to harm your snake's belly. If artificial grass is used it is best practice to have multiple pieces cut to fit the floor of the vivarium. This allows for you to rotate the flooring when needed to clean and dry the other pieces.

Substrates to Avoid

The following substrates should be avoided due to the fact that they are either toxic or indigestible: cedar shavings, gravel, kitty litter, pesticides and fertilizer.

HEATING EQUIPMENT

Corn snakes are cold blooded and therefore rely on their surroundings to get heat. In the wild snakes bask in the sun to keep warm and stay cool by either moving to shady spots of going underground in a mammal burrow or termite hole. Due to this all species of reptile require a temperature gradient within their vivarium to allow them to select a temperature that best suits their individual needs at any given moment. It is important to optimize both temperature and lighting to create a comfortable habitat for your corn snake.

Ceramic Heater

Heat should be provided through a ceramic heater with a pulse thermostat and bulb guard. Ceramic heaters create a good air temperature which is preferred by the corn snake. Ceramic heaters also tend to create ambient lighting which is again preferred by the snake. Ceramic heaters should be set up on one side of your vivarium to allow your corn snake to thermo-regulate. A ceramic bulb can be purchased from any reptile shop. The wattage of the ceramic bulb needed is dependent on the size of the vivarium you are trying to heat – it is best to ask the clerk at the reptile shop for advice on this to tailor the bulb to your specific vivarium.

Under Tank Heater

It is considered best practice to use an under tank heater (such as the 'Zoo Med Repti Therm U.T.H'). Under tank heaters come in various sizes which allows you to choose the best one to create a temperature gradient within your vivarium. It is likewise important to have a decent thermometer available to check the temperature gradient within your vivarium. It is best practice to use a thermometer which is not fixed to the side of the vivarium. By attaching the thermometer to a wall of the vivarium you will only be measuring the temperature of the air within the tank rather and the temperature of the actual surfaces your snake resides on. Hot rocks and heat stones are an alternative method of heating your snake's vivarium. Hot rocks and heat stones are NOT considered best practice for heating a reptile vivarium due to the fact that they can potentially become too hot which can lead to the reptile burning themselves. The optimal temperature gradient for a vivarium containing a corn snake is between 75 degrees Fahrenheit at the cooler end and 88 degrees Fahrenheit at the warmer end (or between 25 and 31 degrees Celsius).

Using a Lightbulb as a Heater

It is common for people to also use regular light

bulbs to supply heat to their snake's vivarium. However they are not as efficient as they require always being turned on. Corn snakes do not need 24 hours of light and a constantly lit bulb could cause anxiety for the snake. It is therefore advisable to invest in a ceramic heater or an under tank heater if you are serious about caring for your snake as they do not cause any form of light-stress. However using a lightbulb as a secondary heating source, in the form of a 20-75 watt incandescent bulb in a ceramic case, is a great way to create an area in the vivarium for your snake to bask. When a bulb is being used as a secondary heat source it is best to place a large flat stone or a thick branch underneath it to allow your snake to bask comfortably.

Bulb Guard

It is vital to have a bulb guard attached to your heater. Snakes do not feel heat in the same way as humans and may not actually realise if they are being burnt by what they are touching. A bulb guard will ensure that your corn snake will stay a safe distance away from the potentially burning bulb.

Brumation

Brumation is a natural energy saving process and is common within adult corn snakes during the cooler months. It serves a very similar purpose to hibernation. Brumation is triggered by a reduction in temperature. Corn snakes will normally eat less, be less active and sleep more during this process and it is best practice to closely monitor your snake during this time.

DISEASE AND ILLNESS

In order to properly care for you snake it is important to be highly observant for signs and symptoms of illness. Often symptoms are not apparent until well into the course of the illness and it is therefore important to promptly address any signs of illness that you notice. Corn snakes are overall hardy animals and they do not have any unique species specific problems. If you have any concerns about your pets health it is best to seek advice from a veterinarian. Below are some common symptoms to look out for.

Stretching and 'Star Gazing'

If you notice that your snake is lying stretched out or has its head raised (commonly termed 'Star Gazing') for a prolonged period of time it could suggest a respiratory infection and its strange posture could indicate that it is uncomfortable. Serious health concerns, such as paramyxovirus and neurological diseases, can be indicated by 'Star Gazing.'

Soaking

Corn snakes are not known for spending a lot of time in water except for when they are trying to help along the shedding process. If your snake is spending an excessive amount of time in its water dish it could indicate that it has mites or that it is having problems thermo-regulating.

Breathing Difficulties

Prolonged stress or exposure to pathogens can cause respiratory illnesses in corn snakes. Respiratory infections can cause wheezing, labored breathing or mucus to be produced out the snakes nose. Respiratory problems can be easily fixed if they are caught early but can likewise quickly turn lethal if left uncheck.

Skin Problems

Minor skin injuries will heal themselves within a shed or two and therefore require no special treatment. Major injuries should be treated with veterinary care. Corn snakes can develop sepsis. Sepsis is characterised by blisters filled with clear fluid and should be immediately treated with veterinary care as it is a serious malady. Sepsis can be avoided by having good, dry and warm conditions within the vivarium.

Anorexia

As previously mentioned corn snakes can be notoriously difficult to feed. There are a plethora of mundane reasons as to why a corn snakes may refuse a meal. However refusal of a meal could suggest that the snake has parasites or an infection. If you become worried about your snake's refusal of food, or if it loses a significant amount of weight, seek veterinary care.

Lumps

Lumps under the skin can mean multiple different things, none of which can be diagnosed without the specialist knowledge of a veterinarian. If your snake has recently eaten any abnormal lumps may be due to the digestion of the meal as it moves through the snake's system. However lumps can also indicate broken bones, abscesses, tumors or parasites. If the lumps are not associated with feeding seek veterinary care.

Activity Patterns

Many new owners are concerned by their snakes lack of movement within the day light hours. Corn snakes are mainly nocturnal and in the wild spend the day in mammal burrows or termite mounds. Therefore there is no reason to worry if your snake spends most of the day curled up or hidden within one of the hides within the vivarium.

FINAL THOUGHTS

Thank you for purchasing our pet care manual on caring for a corn snake. We hope you have found the information both interesting and informative. We hope that this book has allowed you to make an informed choice on whether owning a corn snake suits you and if so we hope that the information will help you to provide the best quality care for your pet corn snake.

We will be publishing multiple other pet care manuals on our author page on Kindle. If you have an interest in exotic and exciting pets then we highly suggest you check out our other work.

I am passionate about providing the best quality information to our customers. We would highly appreciate any feedback, or reviews, you could leave us on our Kindle page to allow us to help create the best possible pet care products available on the market.

Printed in Great Britain
by Amazon

39509770R00030